# The Grind

*Lessons from the Past, Wisdom for the Present*

Simon Obas

ISBN-10:1523448148
ISBN-13:978-1523448142

*For Pierre and Marie Obas who believed!*

*For my family who triumphed!*

# CONTENTS

# ACKNOWLEDGMENTS

I always told myself that if I ever won an award, I'd start off by thanking my Lord and Savior, Jesus Christ. Although this book isn't an award, it is a huge accomplishment and I would be remiss if I didn't acknowledge my creator. Without His love, protection, guidance and direction, I, and hence this book, would not be. Praise God, from Whom all blessings flow.

I cannot thank my mom and dad enough for their unconditional love and support. They instilled in me the values that have transformed me into the man I am today. They are my heroes and I owe all my success to them. No gift can repay all the sacrifices they've made to ensure my siblings and I had a good life. Thank you Mom and Dad!

Many thanks to each and every one of my brothers and sisters. This book is a testament that all things are possible, even when your last name is

Obas. We've been through tough times as a family, but we've always come out stronger. If given the opportunity to have been raised in a wealthier family that was trial and tribulation free, I wouldn't accept the offer. Magalie, Margarete, P, Donly, Abdoula, Emmanuel, Mike, Rachel-I love you! To Mike, my big brother, it was you and me for a while. We've seen each other at our worst and best. You inspire me more than you'll ever know. Thank you! Mono, you taught me so much about what it means to walk like I own the earth. You are the only individual I know who could wear a bright yellow shirt, camouflage pants and orange Timberlands and still be the *flyest* on the block. I get my confidence from you. I love you and I wish you were still here! I'll see you soon!

To my line brothers, Kenny, Vance, Rashad, Joe, Justin, Zeek, JT and Jermaine, who embarked with me on a glorious journey during the spring semester of 2008. I am unapologetically, absolutely, positively honored to call you my brothers and thank you for your unwavering support. Let's continue marching onward and upward, breaking barriers, and living this African-American dream! #DreamTeam #9SultansOfAPhrozenDynasty #Spr08 #JCSU #AO

Malcolm and Fred-THANK YOU! Keith-you inspire all of us younger brothers to strive for greatness! Durrell, Tariq, Herb, Walter, Romar, Rob,

G Means, Germaine, Tristan, Brandon, Black, T. Guess, Marquise, Levar, Tyrell, Dylan, Rob, Ju, Frost, Tone, Ernest, Creighton, Vernell and Dez, Thank You! #AO

Much love to my alma mater, Johnson C. Smith University. One of the best decisions I ever made was to attend this prestigious institution. I learned so much about myself and met some pretty outstanding individuals. It is here I truly learned how powerful, and what it means to be African-American.

#GoldenBulls #YancyEra #Smithite #SmithMade

A heartfelt thank you to my brothers Jeff, Mike Sainte and Chauncy. I was seventeen years old when I met you three. Twelve years later, our friendship is still strong and I appreciate you for always being honest and pushing me to do better. Kristen, the home girl of our crew, thank you for your love, encouragement, and always believing in me. Zena, you have no idea how you've influenced my life. I am so thankful for you. Shawdawn and Malisa, I am grateful for your support over the years. I also want to acknowledge Dr. Walker and Professor King for their contribution to my growth. There are so many other people from JCSU who have supported me in one way or another—you know who you are and I thank you!

To Miles: RIP, Young King!

Much LOVE and RESPECT to my city of Danbury. Thank you to all of my friends both past and present: Travon, Roman, Lawrence and Daryll. No matter where you are, I carry you in my heart! Wanda and Buck, Mamas and Big Black-thank you for opening your home and treating me like a son. Cristal and Pam, words can't express what you mean to me. I thank you for supporting me in everything I do and I am truly lucky to have such loving, caring individuals in my corner. Alexius, you are one of my greatest inspirations. Thank you for everything!

Thank you to my fifth-grade teacher Mrs. Hinckley for igniting a passion for writing inside me. You made me feel valued and pushed me to be the best I could be. Thank you to my high school biology teacher Mr. Calhoun, who was a role model for many of my peers. You showed me what it means to be a fearless African-American

Man. I always knew there was a deeper reason why we clicked. Coach Pardalis, thank you for making me work harder and challenging me every time I set foot on the basketball court. More importantly, thank you for showing me that my actions *off the court* mattered more. Thank you to the HORD Foundation for giving me a scholarship to help pay for college. Thank you to Sandel, Andre, Greg Snopkoski, John Weir, Matt Green, Nyron, Esdras, the Alcide family, and the Harambee Center.

Mr. and Mrs. Dinardo-THANK YOU!!!!! Reverend Pitts-THANK YOU!

To the AFBA class of 2012, you gave me the confidence to pursue a career in education. You taught me so much and I miss you all dearly. #TheRoseThatGrewFromConcrete. Challa, thank you for believing in me. #Lions

Sam-you took a chance and gave me an opportunity of a lifetime. I thank you. I appreciate you. I'm honored to work under your leadership and I'm excited to see our school grow. #CHSLSJ Debon and George, thank you for being positive role models in my life. Aunt Gwen, thank you for always supporting Lenore and I. Mama Brower, thank you for your

greatest creation. She's in good hands-don't worry! Thank you for believing in me and giving me a chance. I love you.

Beside every King is his Queen. Lenore, you are my gorgeous and intelligent lady and I love you very much. Thank you for supporting me, believing in me, and making me a better person. You see the behind the scenes and deal with my craziness. I couldn't have completed this book without you #UMakeMeBetter. I am looking forward to spending the rest of my life with you!

Many more people have contributed to my development and I would run out of paper if I named every one. Nonetheless, I am grateful to all of you. Lastly, thank YOU for taking the time to read this book.

**More life, more peace, more love to each and every one of you.**

# THE GRIND

# Introduction

My name is Simon.

I am a human being. Just like you. I'm also a person who, like you, works hard and has goals that I want to achieve. Growing up, I have noticed that most people do work hard all of their lives. They go to school, get jobs, put in eight to twelve hours a day, get married, and raise families. Many people work even more once they start having kids, just to ensure their children have enough to eat and clothes to wear. These behaviors seem to be the norm wherever I look, whether it's in this country or elsewhere. Some may call it working hard or taking care of business, but I refer to this as "the grind."

People fall into a pattern, get complacent, and barely pursue their dreams. They might have goals in the back of their minds, but once they get caught up in a particular routine, they become resigned to the idea and they can never escape it. Any dreams or goals they might have had when they were younger become unachievable once they feel stuck in life's never-ending monotony. They can't break away and try to accomplish something outside of their predictable lives because they don't think that they have the time or the money to do so.

I'm writing this book with the hope that it will inspire people who have dreams and goals that they want to achieve, but who feel that they can't pursue them for one reason or another. I want to let them know that they can accomplish anything regardless of their circumstance. I want them to know that they can have a new life even if they currently think that they can't.

I have dreams and goals just like you and I have accomplished many of them in my short life so far. Let me name a few; I am a founding Assistant Principal at a New York City high school. I have traveled around the world, visiting over 12 different countries. I'm currently pursuing my doctorate in educational leadership and have achieved an income milestone that most would consider successful, all while under the age of thirty. I don't share this with you to boast, as I am well aware that God can take it all away at any time. However, I want you to know that if you dream it, you can make it happen.

I once heard Will Smith say that he's neither better nor smarter than other people; he just knows that he has an exceptional work ethic. When the other guys are sleeping, Will is working. When the other guys are eating, Will is working. He keeps his eyes on the target. Whatever his goal may be, he pursues it with everything that he has. I have lived my life trying to improve and develop my work ethic so that I can reach new heights.

And that is what this book is about. It will show you the simple, timeless principles that I have applied toward achieving my goals and dreams. They are straightforward and uncomplicated concepts that successful people have used throughout the ages. They are lessons that I have learned while on my grind.

# THE GRIND

# Paris

Paris is truly a beautiful city. It's arguably one of the most exquisite places on Earth, especially if you go during the Christmas season with your significant other. They call it, "The City of Light," and when I arrived there last winter, just before Christmas, I understood exactly why.

We saw everything there was to see in Paris, or at least, we thought we did. The *Mona Lisa's* smile was as sweet and mysterious as I had expected it to be. The Louvre overwhelmed our senses with beauty and awe at every turn. We visited the Arc de Triomphe, the Champs-Élysées, the Musée de l'Homme, and most of the other must-see destinations. I'm not sure why, but we saved the Eiffel Tower for Christmas Day.

The Eiffel Tower is a marvel of engineering, and during the holidays, the festive lighting on the structure makes one feel very welcomed. I felt invited into a new world, a world of metal, lights, smiles and warmth, even in the middle of a cold winter. My excitement continued as we entered the monument and started to climb toward the top of the 984-foot landmark. I couldn't tell what exactly it was, but I knew something in my heart and mind was converging into what I would later call my epiphany.

Although I couldn't quite explain my feelings at the time, I knew that that particular Christmas Day was already becoming one of the best I had ever had. Going up the tower felt like I was on my way toward my destiny. And then we saw the ice skating rink. I couldn't believe my eyes; people were ice skating on one of the levels of the Eiffel Tower. It wasn't a huge space, maybe a couple of thousand square feet, but it was incredible to see something so unexpected in such a world-famous monument.

Unexpected or not, we went ice skating right then and there. When the cool breeze brushed my cheeks, I opened my eyes and felt like I could see, really see, for the first time. I saw my Lenore, who looked more fantastically beautiful at that moment than I had ever seen her before. I saw several parents and kids skating and genuinely enjoying themselves. I saw Paris blanketed in a perfect palette of colored lights imaginable, as if it were some well-designed and properly laid-out neighborhood in the heart of downtown heaven. "Wow!" I thought to myself, "I'm in Paris!" Even though I had been there for several days, I was hit in the face with the realization that here I was, ice skating with the woman I loved, in one of the most magnificent landmarks in the middle of one of the most stunning cities on Earth. I thought all of this was my epiphany at first, and it was such a powerful awakening that if that's all there had been, it certainly would have been enough. However, after feeling the cool breeze on my skin and seeing the lights of Paris, I saw myself.

That moment, which probably lasted a minute, if that, was my true epiphany. In that short time, as I felt the frigid air and smelled the fragrances of that great city, I took an inventory of my whole life. My past flashed before me, and I could clearly see all the smiles, tears, joy and happiness, and all the moments both good and bad.

It seemed as though everything flashed through my mind as quick as lightning. I think I was still skating as I was taking it all in; apparently, I'm a pretty good multitasker. With all the images and words going through my head at once, several things became clear to me. I realized how blessed I was, and was thankful for how much I had been able to accomplish. I also realized that my dreams were coming true and that I'd come a long way. I was ecstatically happy for the first time in my life. I hadn't been unhappy, don't get me wrong, but I had just never been that happy before, and never knew anyone could be. It was a sensational feeling to say the least.

One thought that whizzed through my mind was that I was in Paris, France, three thousand miles from home. It also occurred to me that I could now afford to go to Europe or anywhere else for that matter, whenever I wanted to. The fact that I was ice skating in the Eiffel Tower let me know that all things are possible, even for children of color who come from humble beginnings. It was on that ice skating rink that I truly understood that traveling to experience a whole different culture on a different continent was not farfetched. This was and always will be attainable. That trip to Paris was just a microcosm of the things that I could do. If I wanted to, I could make anything happen. I just needed to grind to do so!

That moment in the Eiffel Tower showed me many things. I saw all of my hard work come to fruition, and it motivated me to strive higher. I knew in that brief burst of time that I had all of the confidence and persistence that I would ever need to attain any goal. It also made me say to myself, "if this is the result of setting goals and going after them, then as soon as I get back to the hotel, I'm going to set more goals and get busy!" Because I've taken the time to set goals, I have successfully achieved a good amount for a man under the age of thirty.

There isn't one set definition for success. It

means different things to different people. Ask your friends what it means and each individual will give you a slightly different answer. Success is relative. For me, to be successful is not about having the most money or cars or houses. Success is about accomplishing the goals that you set and doing something good with your life.

However, before you can succeed, you must have an idea of where you are going and what you want. Creating goals, as cliché as it sounds, is the most powerful thing you can do to succeed. Often, human beings underestimate the power of setting goals and as a result, they do not accomplish anything. They end up going in circles and wasting time. The years go by, and they find themselves stagnant and unhappy.

In the following chapters, I draw on different parts of my life to illustrate how I have achieved success through my grind. None of this is rocket science; it's quite simple. I hope that the steps I mention will inspire you to set goals and chase after your dreams. No gimmicks, no riddles; just simple steps that complement each other. Without further ado, allow me to introduce my story to you!

# THE GRIND

# The Power of Belief

*I always felt like I could do anything. That's the main thing people are controlled by; thoughts and perceptions of themselves.*

*-Kanye West*

How many of us believe in ourselves? If we thought about it, we could probably answer that question, but most of us would lie about it. Is that too harsh? Maybe, but it's true. So, let's turn that question into a statement. Instead of "Do I believe in myself?" let's just say, "I believe in myself!" Yes, exclamation point and all. Saying "I believe in myself!" is a powerful thing indeed.

When you say this very positive affirmation to yourself, you are telling or rather commanding yourself to believe in you. You are telling your "self" that you are someone of worth and value. If you continue to tell yourself that you are a valuable human being, you will start believing it. And then soon after that, you will begin to act as if you are someone who is worthy and valuable. And the next logical thing to happen is that other people will see you in that same light.

Now, this phrase may seem like four simple words strung together to make a declarative sentence. But those words, when repeated continuously throughout the day, day after day, are equivalent to getting a great workout in the gym. If you start working out regularly, your muscles get bigger, your health improves, and your endurance and strength increase more than you would have ever expected.

The first step in achieving your goals is believing in yourself. It gives you the endurance and strength of mind to maintain your progress when pursuing your dreams. You need confidence when you start, and you will need it as you move forward. Remember, achieving what you want will take more than a day, especially if you have long-term or larger goals in mind. Believing in yourself 24/7 takes a little practice and a little time each day to perfect.

Case in point, when I was going to college, I had to believe in myself every minute of every single day. Obstacles were thrown at me from every conceivable angle, and the opportunity to quit was laid at my feet several times. Many people lose faith in themselves and find it easier to go back to what they were doing before. I wanted a college education more than anything at that time, so I had to believe in myself.

Of course, just because you believe in yourself doesn't mean that things will get easier. I vividly remember my struggles with money when I first started college. I didn't receive much financial aid, so I was a part-time student throughout my first three semesters of school. Unfortunately, by the end of my third semester, I had a huge financial balance that had to be paid off before I could take my final exams and start my fourth semester. So I was forced to take a semester off of school, go back home and get three jobs so that I could pay off my balance. This was the beginning of the grind!

Although I am the second-to-last of ten kids and have two incredible parents, I did not have a college trust fund. My parents emigrated from Haiti in the late '80s, and neither had an American education. Their English skills were pretty limited, and they got jobs as cleaning staff in a hotel in downtown Miami that paid $3 an hour. As time went on, they found different kinds of work, but together, they made no more than $60,000 annually during my childhood. My parents didn't have any money, but they had plenty of love to give and taught me life lessons that I will share with you throughout this book.

In what should have been my fourth semester in college, I worked as a sales associate at the Gap, a car lot attendant at Saturn, and a custodian at a local pharmaceutical company. It was steady work, and I familiarized myself with the retail industry, learned how to drive a stick shift, and became the best floor buffer on the planet. But the biggest lesson I learned during this time was that not everyone will believe in you, and therefore, you must believe in yourself. I had to learn this the hard way.

After discussing an idea that I had to raise money to go back to school with some fellow employees, I decided to make an appointment with the CEO to gain his approval. If I could get the CEO of this large pharmaceutical corporation that I worked for to believe in my dreams and award me this opportunity, then this could potentially be my ticket back to school. I figured I had nothing to lose, but my job. My idea was that since I was doing such a great job in my custodial position, then perhaps he wouldn't mind requesting one dollar from each of his employees to donate to my college fund. Since there were hundreds of workers spread across the company, I thought that no one would mind donating a buck to a nineteen-year old, African-American kid who was trying to get a higher education.

After presenting my idea clearly and concisely, I smiled and waited for an answer. He stared at me with an unreadable look on his face and then he wrote something on a notepad and put his pen down. I still couldn't read his face as he continued to look me in the eye. I don't even think he blinked the whole time he was glaring at me.

My smile began to fade a bit, and it was then that he lifted his arm, stretched it out, and pointed his index finger at the door. I looked at the door and then looked back at him. I thought he was just joking when he said, "There's the door." But apparently, he wasn't, because I got a call later that evening from some nameless, disembodied voice assuring me that the company no longer required my services. It happened so fast that I was momentarily stunned, but then, I got off the phone and started planning my next move. I can't blame him, I suppose, but I was surprised when he said, "You're fired!" Was it my suggestion or the way I had presented it? I may never know because I'm not going back to ask him, and I'm tired of trying to figure it out.

Even after that experience, the belief that I had in myself never wavered. Why? Because regardless of being terminated when I asked for help, I still held on to my dream. I wanted to get back into college, and I wouldn't let anyone get in the way of that. I realized that not everyone will believe in you and your dreams as much as you do. Therefore, it is imperative that you believe in yourself. If I didn't believe in myself, who would? No one, certainly not the CEO of a company that held no future for me anyway. Why would I let someone like that ruin my harmony or make me stop believing in my ability to achieve my goals?

Obstacles like this one pop up all of the time to challenge your confidence and the way you perceive yourself. Remember, you are worthy, and your goals are invaluable. You have to believe in yourself because there are people who want to see you fail. That CEO believed in himself, that's for sure, and perhaps, he was threatened by my audacity to do whatever it took to succeed. Why let people like him ruin your day, let alone your dreams and your sense of self? I am not mad at the CEO, and I wish him the best. His "no" pushed me even harder to pursue my goal in getting back to JCSU and completing my college career. When people say no to you, don't speak ill of them; instead, thank them for making you believe in yourself that much more.

I could have easily decided to stay in Connecticut and attend a local college, receive state financial aid, and have fewer monetary challenges. But that wasn't what I wanted. I was motivated to finish off where I started and because I said it in my head, it was already done! Now, I just had to find a way to grind and actually get it done.

One method for believing in yourself is to figure out the *purpose* of what you are trying to accomplish. No one in my family graduated from college. I witnessed firsthand, how hard life is for an individual without a degree, especially if you are an African-American. With this understanding, I knew that for me to accomplish all of the many things that I had in mind, the first step was for me to graduate from college. So I had to believe I could get accepted into college, complete my four years of course work and earn my bachelor's degree. As you pursue your dreams, remember that the first step is to believe in yourself. Look in the mirror and ask yourself, "Why do I want this?" Dig deep and find the purpose to stay motivated! There's no room for self-doubt when you are on the grind. Self-doubt can destroy your dreams and your ability to accomplish your goals faster than ever before.

You have to have intrinsic motivation when the odds are against you. I'm sure that you have heard the idiom, "Anything that's worth having is worth fighting for." When obstacles present themselves, you have to face them, put your dukes up, and bob and weave. I believe in my dreams because I know my worth. If I had any room for self-doubt, I would have thrown in the towel after I got fired from my custodial position back in 2005. All I asked for was a little help in the form of a dollar, and I got the boot. However, giving up wasn't an option, and I wasn't about to start doubting my ability to accomplish my goal.

By the way, I recently ran into that CEO, who fired me. We briefly caught up and exchanged contact information. As I was leaving, he asked me if I could participate as a panelist for a diversity workshop he was coordinating. I smiled and said *I believed* I was busy that day, and that I would be in touch.

# Set Goals

*Setting goals is the first step in turning the invisible into the visible.*

*-Tony Robbins*

So what happens once you believe in yourself? You set goals, of course. The thing to remember is that you are always in charge of setting goals for your life. No one else ever really does it for you. When I was in sixth through eighth grade, I tried out for the basketball team each season. And every season, I was cut after tryouts. All of my friends were on the team, but for some reason, I just couldn't make the roster. I thought that I was a good player, but couldn't figure out why I was the only one who didn't make the team year after year.

I never gave up or got discouraged. Each year, I became more determined to make the basketball team. It became my goal and a bit of an obsession. When I got to Danbury High School, which was the largest secondary school in the state, there were more talented players to compete with, but knowing that only made me work harder. I had to get on my grind because the competition was real! I had tenacity and grit, and I never let the bigger guys or the better athletes intimidate me. My goal was to make the team, and I worked toward that goal each and every day.

I set smaller goals to develop my athletic skills so that I could attain my bigger goal of making the team. I challenged myself to practice for an hour and a half each day. I increased the amount of lay-ups and jump shots that I would need to complete daily so that I could become a more efficient offensive player. I challenged myself to run twenty suicides every day to build my endurance and stamina. I knew that achieving these smaller goals daily would enable me to do my best on tryout day and potentially make the team.

I would sneak into the local state university to use their gym to practice. I was often kicked out by the security guards because I was not a student at their institution, but I kept going back to try and perfect my craft as a baller. I watched films of basketball games and played them over and over in my head, replacing the great players' faces with my own. I even prayed about basketball. I didn't ask God to specifically get me on the team, but I did ask Him to be with me while I practiced and during tryouts.

The week of the tryouts during my freshman year of high school finally came, and I gave it my all. I worked harder than ever before and continued to believe that I would make the team. A few days later, the news was posted: Yes, I had made the team! Goal accomplished. I use this story to illustrate the importance of setting goals. Just the act of consciously setting a goal fuels your motivation. It empowers you in a way that is unlike anything else. You give *yourself* the power to make things happen in *your* life.

You can have long-term goals, short-term goals, or intermediate goals, it doesn't matter. Any goal you decide to set is one that you must take seriously. It's not an efficient use of time to set meaningless goals or objectives only to eventually veer from the path and not achieve them. Many people do this and rationalize their actions by saying the goal was meaningless anyway. If it was worthless, then why set it at all? Don't set useless goals. Move on and pursue only things that have real meaning to you.

This doesn't mean that each goal you set must be monumental. Goals come in all shapes and sizes, and you should examine them before making a commitment. Figure out how to prioritize the attainment of your goals. Take the time out to think through your goals before you commit to them. So you want to be successful? That's a worthy goal, but how exactly are you going to attain that goal? Perhaps you want to be a lawyer on Wall Street, but you first need to get your law degree and pass the bar exam. Or maybe you wish to be a world-renowned chef, but you first need to complete culinary classes and perfect your cooking skills.

Whatever it is, you have to be specific about what you wish to accomplish. This will allow your goals to feel attainable and not so far-fetched. As you gain small wins along the way, you will have more self-esteem, which, in turn, will give you greater motivation to chase your dreams. The big win is sweet and is what you should aim to achieve, but it is the small victories throughout the process that matter most. Setting measurable goals will allow you to act with intent and purpose.

When I wanted to be on the basketball team, I knew it would take a lot of practice and a great deal of effort. I also committed to that goal knowing that achieving it wasn't guaranteed, no matter how much I practiced and how hard I tried. The only noticeable element in my work toward the goal was that I could observe that I was becoming a better player. After a few weeks of continual practice, I noticed that my legs were stronger, I could run faster and farther, and I could make more jump shots and lay-ups than before. Those were all measurable factors in moving toward my goal. The only thing that wasn't measurable was whether or not I would get on the team after all that hard work.

Achieving that major milestone taught me a lot. I learned that just setting a large goal is not enough; you have to work hard at setting and attaining those smaller goals in order to get there. If you want to be an actor, you must go on auditions, know your character and practice your lines in front of the mirror—every day. Every single day, you must grind and go at it. You must have total commitment to your smaller goals. Set the goals, grind, never give up or doubt yourself. You can totally achieve them if you commit to all of your goals.

# It's Time

*Time = Life, Therefore, waste your time and waste your life, or master your time and master your life.*

*-Alan Lakein*

How can you achieve your goals if you don't have the time? That is a fair question that most of us ask. My answer is simple: if you don't have the time, make some. I know that you are probably thinking, easier said than done. After I graduated from college and started teaching, I wanted to get a master's degree. In order to make time for that goal, I would have to work 5 ten-hour days, and then devote 6 hours to coursework. Needless to say, this did not account for time that I would spend completing homework. I was also coaching a boys' varsity basketball team. I had a lot of different commitments to follow through on, with what felt like very little time.

At first, I asked myself, how the heck am I going to juggle these three, time-consuming activities? I started to make excuses for why I could not and should not, but then I realized that excuses are tools of the incompetence. I understood that if I didn't get a master's degree, I wouldn't be able to progress in my career, which meant that I wouldn't accomplish my long-term goals. I had to take control of the situation. If I wanted to pursue my dreams, I either needed to magically make more hours in the day and survive on about half the amount of sleep that I was getting per night, or organize my time in a manner that would allow me to work, attend grad school, do my homework, coach basketball, and have a *life*.

Part of the key to success is having an efficient work ethic. The cousin of good work ethic is time management. I simply went through my daily activities and prioritized which things I could do at specific times on a daily basis. I created an entirely new schedule that enabled me to do everything I was doing previously and get my master's degree in a much more efficient way.

Once I figured out how to virtually add more hours to the day, I was less overwhelmed and gained a peace of mind. You do have to be careful with this, especially if you don't want your life to become too regimented. Don't forget to schedule some fun recreational time for yourself. You will need this "me time" to relax and wind down. "Me time" is an important element in achieving your goals. It reminds you that there is more to life than work and will help you to put your goals back into perspective.

After you have successfully integrated organization and time management into your daily regimen, you will begin to feel more self-confidence and a sense of empowerment over your life. You chose the goal, believed in yourself enough to commit to pursuing it, and have begun to allocate the appropriate time to achieve those goals. These consciously determined moves can change everything— forever. It will certainly change your perception of how attainable your goals truly are.

You will have a brand-new awareness of life and where you and your goals fit into it.

Sean Combs, also known as Puffy, took a train from DC to NYC every weekend to intern for Uptown Records, while he was an undergrad at Howard University. He could have made excuses as to why he could not or should not do it, but he didn't. So for those of you out there who insist you don't have time, I'm here to let you know that you can make time for whatever you truly believe in. Whenever you make an excuse, you are jeopardizing your goals. Every excuse is time wasted. Time is the most valuable resource, so use it!

While writing this book, I am currently pursuing my doctoral degree while simultaneously co-founding and running a high school in New York City. Do you know the amount of work that goes into starting a school from scratch? Talk about time management! To keep all of these things in balance and running smoothly, I have to make sure that my priorities are in order and that time management is at the forefront of my mind.

It is a juggling act, but it can be done. This is not miraculous stuff we're talking about here, but when you organize your time to chase your dreams, your whole life will change for the better. When you make time to work towards your goals, you are saying, not only to yourself but also to the world that you have deep desires and ambitions that will allow you to reach your full potential.

We have all heard the phrase, "time is of the essence." It's an idiom used in contract law that lets the parties involved know that a task must be completed on or before a certain date. The beautiful thing about achieving a personal goal is that you are the judge of when you must accomplish it. Your goal may be a long-term one that could take several years to complete, like getting your bachelor's or master's degree over the course of several years. Other goals will be shorter and will require less time to achieve them.

In case you haven't been paying attention to the news, tomorrow is never promised. I have witnessed many of my friends neglect making time to achieve their goals because things come up, and they say they will get to them later. Unfortunately, later never gets here. Prioritize your goals and make it happen! Have kids? Have the other parent watch them or use a babysitter. Don't have a car? Take a cab or the bus. Don't have Wi-Fi? Invest in a free library account where you can access Wi-Fi. Got dreams? Organize your time and achieve them!

# Visualize

*I would visualize things coming to me. It would just make me feel better. Visualization works if you work hard. That's the thing. You can't just visualize and then go eat a sandwich.*

*-Jim Carey*

I started visualizing my future at a young age. It helped me to see my goals clearly and understand that I could achieve them. When I wanted to attain something, I simply visualized it happening, and that started me on the road to achievement. Once I saw myself accomplishing a goal in my mind, it was much easier to make it happen in real life. Without knowing how powerful this tool was, I used it to move forward in life and to get where I wanted to be.

What is visualization? We have all heard the word before, but what does it mean in relation to attaining your goals? Basically, in this context, it is the act of consciously seeing yourself succeeding at something you want to accomplish. For instance, anytime I set my mind on something, I "watch" myself attain it. Until I graduated from college, I visualized myself every single day, walking across the stage and receiving my diploma. I did the same thing when I was working on my master's degree. Now that I am in a Doctoral program, I visualize myself receiving that degree in front of an applauding audience. I also visualize people calling me Dr. Obas.

This is not a fairytale imagining; it is scientifically proven to work. A few years ago, an Australian psychologist named Alan Richardson, completed a famous study on sports visualization. He had a large group of basketball players each shoot a hundred baskets from the foul line and recorded their numbers, and then he split them up into three smaller random groups. The first group was given the task of shooting baskets from the foul line for twenty minutes each day for five days a week over the course of four weeks.

The second group was asked to do nothing physical in the same amount of time. They were even instructed not to think about basketball. The third group was instructed to come to the basketball court and be guided through a visualizing process of shooting baskets for twenty minutes each day for five days a week over the course of four weeks. However, the catch for the third group was that they were never to touch a basketball. Everything they did was to be done in their minds.

After four weeks, the three groups each shot one hundred baskets again, and the results of the study came in. The first group, which had practiced shooting basketballs, had improved their skills, and the actual number of shots in the basket had increased by 24%. The second group, which had done absolutely nothing related to basketball, had no increase in skills or the number of baskets made. The third group, which had never touched a basketball but had visualized making baskets from the foul line, had improved in skills and the number of baskets made by 23%. That is incredible! By simply concentrating on visualizing the baskets going into the hoop, the third group had improved nearly as much as the first group who was practicing drills that entire time. The mind is a powerful tool indeed!

When I visualize, I concentrate on the result I want to see happen. Let me rephrase that: when I visualize, I concentrate on the result I intend to see happen. I see myself walking across the stage to receive my diploma, but at the same time, I insist that this will happen so that it comes to fruition. Visualization isn't widely accepted in the sports world or in any other field for that matter. Even though it's been consistently shown to produce effective results, people just don't buy it.

Perhaps visualization is too far ahead of its time. And perhaps I feel sorry for those who could be even more successful if they had just visualized, but who instead, just dismissed this concept as useless. So, with that being said, I challenge you to visualize your goals and success because it works! Aside from the group of basketball players mentioned above, this concept has worked for many world-class athletes, including Tiger Woods; basketball legends; Larry Bird, Jerry West and Michael Jordan; and baseball great Roy Halladay. They worked out, practiced and used **every** tool they could to be the best. Visualization just happens to be one of those tools.

You will get even more out of this technique if you engage all of your senses. So, for instance, when I visualize myself walking across the stage and receiving my doctoral degree, I can hear the audience applauding and smell the auditorium. When I reach out and take my diploma, I can feel the texture of the rolled-up document in my hand. I can feel the warmth and the pressure of the dean's handshake. I can also feel my smile grow wider and wider as I look out into the audience and see the joy illuminating from my parent's faces. I can feel all of the emotions that I will experience when I actually do walk across that stage. When you use all of your senses, you are using your entire self through the visualization process, and that means you are totally committed to making the achievement of your goal a reality.

I came from humble beginnings, and I visualized myself escaping my situation and being successful. Something that made the visualization process, even more, powerful was looking in the mirror and verbally affirming my goals. Some may think that standing in front of a mirror and talking to yourself is strange, but I believe it is empowering. Great speakers, preachers, political debaters and news commentators do it several times a day. They are not only rehearsing their speeches, but are actually visualizing how they will present themselves when they get out in front of the audience. I do it often because this is a great way to reinforce my visualization.

Some may call it having an imagination, which is

fine, and some may see a deeper meaning to the use of visualization. Imagination does come into play when you start visualizing, but when you get used to doing it, it becomes second nature and a part of your daily routine. I told myself a long time ago that if I wanted to achieve something, no matter what it was, I would allow myself to use whatever tools were available to me. Visualization, I have to say, is one of the most important tools I have found thus far.

# Failure Is Feedback

*I've missed more than 9,000 shots in my career. I've lost almost 300 games. Twenty-six times, I've been trusted to take the game-winning shot and missed. I've failed over and over and over again in my life. And that is why I succeed.*

*-Michael Jordan*

I've discovered that when I think positively about events that I have labeled failures, they don't look so bad after all. Retrospectively, these failures become valuable learning experiences. Now I don't mean that I just pretend that a failure or a setback never happened, instead, when I experience something that I might call a failure, I assess what took place, analyze my actions and reactions, and learn from it in every way possible. Failure is feedback; it should always reveal critical information that you can learn from.

A failure is letting you know that whatever it was that you did or went through should not be done again, or in certain instances, done the same way. It took me a long time to understand that it is okay to fail, as long as you learn from it. The best of us have had various failures in our lives. Big ones, little ones—failures and difficulties can derail us at times, and we often cannot avoid them. No matter how well we proactively plan, some things are just out of our control. In these situations, we must adjust our reactions and productively bounce back from our failures.

During my senior year in college, when I was twenty-two, I applied for a job at Teach for America. TFA is a non-profit organization that recruits college graduates to teach in economically depressed communities for two years at a time. I wanted that to be my first job after I graduated from college because I believed in their mission and knew that it would be an amazing opportunity to get my roots planted in education. I had all of the confidence in the world that they would love me and see my potential. I went through the application process, went through an in-depth interview, and left their office knowing that I would get a call from them in the upcoming days asking when I could start.

A week had passed, and I didn't hear anything from them. Another week went by and again, not a word. Finally, at the beginning of the third week, I received an e-mail from one of the recruiters that I had worked with throughout the application process. When I started reading the email, I couldn't believe my eyes. It was a formal letter thanking me for my application, but informing me that I would not be receiving an offer to be a part of that year's cohort. I was stunned and disappointed. I just knew that I was going to get that offer, but received a rejection notice instead.

Six years later, I am a founding administrator of a high school in the largest school district in the United States. How did that happen? Up to this day, I still don't know why I didn't get hired to be a corps member with Teach for America, and at this point, I don't care. I stopped worrying about it a few hours after I read the rejection email. A few hours was all I needed to regroup, recognize my feelings at the moment, analyze my actions and the situation that I considered to be a failure, and plan my next move. I was going to become a teacher one way or the other, and I wasn't going to let a person or organization hinder me from achieving that goal.

Should I have taken more time to feel sorry for myself or beat myself up wondering about the would'ves, could'ves, should'ves? Many people do take an extended time to feel sorry for themselves and sulk when failures arise, and then they fall behind in their progress. Some people take days, weeks, months or even years to get over a perceived failure. I certainly understand that we are human beings filled with emotion. But taking too much time to weep over something that you cannot fix is not an efficient use of time nor will it change the past or allow for a productive future. Not getting the opportunity to work for Teach for America made me realize that I had to work harder to achieve my goal and that there was a different path that God wanted me to take to get there. I got rejected, which most would deem a failure, but I used that as feedback to add more fuel to the fire that continued to push me forward.

Why do you think sports teams watch videos of the game that they lost the previous week? They do it so that they can learn from their mistakes. The coach points out obvious errors to the players, and then they rewind the tape and watch it a few more times to make sure that they didn't miss anything. They watch their mistakes until they fully understand why and how they failed on a certain play. Once they have analyzed what they did wrong, they create practice drills to ensure that the mistake won't happen again. They use their loss as feedback to improve their craft so that they can win the next game, which is their goal. This is just one example.

Henry Ford had plenty of failures and decided early on to learn from them, instead of letting them ruin his future. His ideas and designs were turned down several times by various individuals, which probably would have made people with less drive give up instantly. Henry Ford, of course, was not the kind of person to quit. When he had a goal, he did not let anything get in his way. When he was rejected from opportunities or his car models failed in some way, he analyzed the problem for feedback and used it to improve and move forward. He never lost faith or took his eyes off of the goal.

Bill Gates dropped out of Harvard and never received his bachelor's degree, which some people might consider to be a failure. He and Paul Allen failed in their first business venture, but fortunately, they learned from their mistakes, improved their product, and continued to work toward their goal. Their goal to build a better and more accessible computer operating system, which is now today's Microsoft.

How about Walt Disney? Did you know that he was fired by a newspaper firm because his boss said he didn't have an imagination? Obviously, there are millions of examples of people who failed and then went on to having very successful lives. The only difference between them and those who let failure ruin their progress is that they decided to learn from their setbacks and to improve. They recognized that failure is part of life and that you simply can't let it win. They all knew that they had to learn from their failures in order to productively move forward. They also knew that once they made a particular mistake and corrected it, they would never make it again. These mindsets and reactions would bring them closer to their goal.

The next time you experience a failure, analyze it and, if possible, determine what went wrong. Go ahead and allow yourself to feel the emotions that you need to feel—but briefly. Then make the necessary corrections and improvements and continue to move toward your goal. Use the feedback to improve now so that you can perform better tomorrow. To start achieving your goals faster, just get into the habit of analyzing your failure, correcting the problem, and moving on.

Many people don't allow themselves to move on because they let the failure consume them and become larger than what it needs to be. You will lose momentum and become demoralized. Once you are demoralized, it becomes difficult to think of your goal as attainable. So once you recognize and learn from your failure, you must regard it as just another life experience that gave you valuable feedback. Many highly successful people end up being grateful for their failures because they made them stronger, smarter and more understanding of their value in correlation to their goals.

# Surround Yourself With Success

*"If every person in your clique is rich, your clique is rugged. Nobody will fall because everyone will be each other's crutches".*

*-Jay Z*

Generally, our parents are the first ones to guide u
away from people they feel aren't good influences ¡
toward the ones that they think would be a more
positive influence on us. When we get older,
however, we are on our own. We have to fend for
ourselves—doing laundry, cooking, paying rent and
necessities, and choosing the people we allow to stay
in our lives. You are right, I did say "choosing". It is
up to us to decide on the individuals who we allow to
remain in our lives. Hopefully, we choose wisely.

The motto of the college that I attended is
"Surround Yourself with Success". My interpretation
of this motto is to always keep people around you
who will add value to your life one way or another.
With that said, you will also have to leave people
behind who are not adding these things to your life,
while on your journey to your goal. And this isn't a
bad thing; it is just another part of life. If you are
writing a term paper and the TV and the radio are
both on as loud as can be, most people would simply
turn at least one, if not both of them off. Why?
Because the loud noises from both devices are a
distraction that is keeping you from achieving your
goal, which is to write that term paper.

People are the same way. Now, this might sound
a bit cold and unfeeling, but just wait until you read
the rest of this chapter before making any judgments.
I feel that it is perfectly okay and warranted to end

friendships; it happens every day all over the world. Once again, it is all a matter of choice. You can have all of the goals in the world, but if you don't take the necessary steps to achieve them, they are just pipe dreams. If a friend is hindering you from achieving your goal, there are only two solutions. One is to stop working towards the goal and keep the friend around, and the other is to go after the goal and to lose the friend. It sounds so easy and simple on paper, doesn't it? To be honest, based on your circumstance, this can be a lot easier said than done.

Remember, we started off this chapter by saying that our parents guide us away from people who were bad influences and toward the ones that they thought would add value to our lives. Now, you have to be the one to make these judgments and to put this into action. I keep the individuals whom I call friends and will help me to become a better person in my life. They are the ones who are driven and on a similar path to success and self-improvement. Have you ever noticed how genuinely good people can bring the best out in other folks? Well, they do, and it is always a pleasure to be around them.

My friend Zena asked me to be a part of the student government association at JCSU when I attended for undergrad. I never saw myself going after a leadership opportunity like that in college, but once I agreed to it, I discovered that it was one of the best decisions that I had ever made. I loved that the opportunity pushed my thinking in different ways and allowed me to develop outside of my comfort zone. Becoming a part of that association in college had never occurred to me until Zena brought it to my attention. That little push from a trusted friend moved me forward in a whole new direction toward success. Zena added a piece of value to my life journey. Although student government was something that happened in college, it taught me many skills that I still use in my career up until this day.

Now it is easy to keep individuals like that in your life, but it can be very difficult to rid yourself of those who either don't contribute or contribute negatively to your life. You can usually sense when a person isn't truly a good friend or if they could potentially pull you in a direction that alters your path to success. Sometimes, we don't heed to the faint warning signals that we get when we are around some of our "friends" because we don't want to or because we believe that they will change. These vague, almost unreadable feelings are similar to the tiny light on our car's dashboard that occasionally comes on and says "check engine" or "check fuel".

Most people act like everything must be okay because the car is running smoothly until a bigger issue arises that causes you to have to deal with that light or signal. Many just ignore the warning and continue with their lives. That's the same way it is with the uncomfortable feelings we get around some of our "friends." We ignore those little warning signals and act as if everything is fine and dandy until we realize that we are either way off track or we have completely abandoned our goal because a "friend" was somehow in the way of it.

Recently, I once ignored my gas light and embarrassingly had my car stop in the middle of busy traffic on 125th and Lenox Avenue in Harlem. My girlfriend had to take a cab to the gas station, fill up a gas container just to get us enough juice to get the car started. It's not that I didn't have money to get gas for my car; I had just decided to ignore the light and keep driving because I didn't want to stop at a gas station. While waiting for her return, I immediately called my line brother Justin, and he laughed saying, "You should have paid attention to the gas light!" *It's the same with those friends who do not add value to your life.* I have learned my lesson, and now without delay, I take my car to get gas when the "check fuel" light comes on.

Sometimes, you will come across friends who will use you, which is even worse. Not only are they not adding any value, but they are feeding off of the wonderful things that you have worked so hard to produce. Years ago, I had a friend who would come around only when he needed something. If he needed money, I was there to shell out a few dollars. If he needed advice, I was there to offer heartfelt suggestions. If he needed something to eat, my food was his food. He was my friend, but the pattern was becoming clear: he only came to me when he needed something. I started to realize that my resources and time were beginning to diminish because I was too busy "looking out". Now the only way that I would consider keeping him in my life is if he would do the same for me. So I decided to start asking for favors to see what his response would be.

When I asked him for a few non-monetary favors, he gave me excuse after excuse and wouldn't help me. After that, our "friendship," as one-sided as it was, was over. I made the decision to end it. Ending that relationship was like a refreshing glass of cold water for me. The moment that I divested myself of that friendship was the moment that I truly felt empowered. The whole process just made me a stronger person, and a smarter one, too. Now, when I see those faint warning signals in my relationships, I examine them closely and act on them.

Now, we really can't blame that *friend* for the abandonment or derailment of our goal because he or she had nothing to do with that decision. We chose, either consciously or subconsciously, to have that individual remain in our life which caused us to become deterred from our goal. We made the wrong decision. Had we acted on those little warning signals, the uncomfortable feelings we had when we were around that person, we could have been much farther along in our grind. However, all is not lost. Even though we have lost a great deal of valuable time, we can still make up for it if we are willing to take immediate action toward reaching our goal.

The first step is to look at the failure or how far off-path you are, analyze what went wrong or who is holding you back. Learn from this failure by committing to choosing to keep **only** the people in your circle who will help you become a better person. That means that the *friend* who somehow, was involved in you not achieving your goal cannot hold the same meaning in your life anymore. It doesn't mean that you must throw rocks at the person or never speak to them again in life.

It simply means that you are now re-prioritizing how much presence certain individuals have in your life so that you can get back on track to achieving your goal. You don't have valuable time to waste anymore. If nothing of substance leading toward your goals is coming out of spending time with that person, then they don't need to be around you as much anymore. It is that simple. God has not ordained everyone to be a part of your final destination.

Once you commit to keeping **only** the people in your circle, who will help you become a better person, you will start to make progress toward your goal again. Rudyard Kipling once wrote, "He travels fastest who travels alone." But we might say here that he travels fastest who travels with people who will help him to excel.

Who's in your inner circle?

# The Power of Self-Discipline

*"Discipline is just choosing between what you want NOW and what you want MOST*

*-Anonymous*

Success is difficult to achieve without discipline. If you happen to look up the word "discipline" in the Merriam-Webster Dictionary, you'll see that it has more than one meaning. It can be used to indicate punishment, a field of study, self-control; a system of rules that governs conduct, training that builds character or perfects the mind, gaining control by enforcing order, and orderly or prescribed conduct or patterns of behavior.

We all have discipline in our lives, whether we know it or not, and I bet that most of us don't even realize that it influences our success and failures every single day. When we get up, brush our teeth, make our bed and breakfast, we are using discipline. Discipline in the sense that we are simply being orderly and following a certain pattern of behavior regularly. That behavior pattern, however we learned it, allows us to carry out our responsibilities and pushes us forward through our daily routines. We may think of it as just the morning routine that we have been doing for years, but it's actually more than that. It has become part of our character, and life would be different for us if we stopped doing these things.

The habits that one develops to have a better and more successful life can't flourish without some form of self-discipline. Some extent of discipline is involved in achieving any goal, no matter how big or small. Discipline enables you to live more efficiently, focus on your goals, and avoid any issues that may arise. Every successful person on Earth is a disciplined human being. Discipline manifests itself differently in every individual. He or she may not look disciplined because their desk is a mess covered in paperwork, but if that person is successful, he or she is disciplined in some way. They have developed habitual behaviors that have enhanced their progress and led them closer to success.

When I was younger, my father taught me to always get my clothes ready for the next day, the night before. He called this being disciplined and saving valuable time the following morning. My mother overheard us talking and chimed in saying, "It's just being organized". I actually believe it's both. It is certainly being organized and disciplined, if you do it regularly. The simple act of preparing something the night before you need it is an amazing time saver. It allows you to be free the next morning to do something more valuable with your time than figuring out which pants, shirt and socks you are going to wear. It may not sound like a big deal, but the cumulative effect on the amount of time and brain power you save is awesome.

Let's say it takes an average of ten minutes to go through your closet and pick out an outfit. Five days of that equals 50 minutes per work week that you have spent each morning. Multiply that by 52 weeks in the year and you have spent a total of 43.3 hours in your closet looking for outfits. That extra 10 minutes in the mornings could have been spent getting to work or school earlier, or even staying in bed. Aside from time, that extra brain power and decision making that you use to figure out what you will wear each day could go into previewing an assignment or checking your email. This is a fascinating way to look at how your accumulated time for an activity is really spent. Self-discipline simply gives you more options for how to use your valuable time.

Being disciplined makes it easier for me to focus on my goals and to use my brain power, decision making and time more efficiently. I have to prioritize my daily activities and be disciplined enough to ensure that I follow through with them. My daily morning routine is the start of my disciplined life. You probably never even thought to call it discipline, but that's exactly what it is.

Do you think being disciplined is easy? Doing your morning tasks, like brushing your teeth, making your bed, etc. took years of practice before becoming second nature. Growing up your parents or guardians most likely nagged and cajoled you every morning to get up and put that toothbrush in your hand. And then one day, you just got up and did it on your own. A solid habit was formed right then and there and a disciplined life began in front of that bathroom sink with that toothbrush.

Creating disciplined habits is possible because as human beings we have great willpower. If our goal is to stop smoking, guess what, we can do it! Millions of people have done it before us and we probably have a few friends who have done it, too. When you quit smoking, you are actually doing two things simultaneously: breaking an old habit and developing a new disciplined habit, which is the deliberate act of not smoking. That's the reason why it is so difficult for smokers to quit because it takes just as much time and hard work, if not more, to break an old habit.

Once you develop self-discipline to establish positive daily habits, you will naturally be able to adjust your schedule to tackle almost any goal. When I ran out of financial aid in college, I had to take on three different jobs which required a lot of discipline. There was never a question of quitting school— graduating was my goal, so I had to shift my priorities and discipline myself in a way to do whatever it took to make enough money to pay my tuition. Once I returned to school, I got another job at Dillard's, a department store selling ladies' shoes. I scheduled everything around school and class assignments, which were my priorities. I knew on which days I had what classes, and about how much homework I would have in each, so I could develop a daily routine. This required discipline. I would always try and do my homework immediately after the class I had instead of procrastinating and putting it off until later. I saved myself a great deal of anxiety while getting through my coursework just by making this disciplined decision.

My parents were incredibly disciplined and I learned a lot through their incredible work ethic. Both of them worked the overnight shift, which meant that they started their jobs at 11:00 p.m. My dad got off at 7:00 a.m. and then went straight to his other job, which started at 8:00 a.m. My mother got off at 7:00 a.m., as well, but she would come home to get us ready for school, make breakfast, drop us off at the bus stop, and then go to her second job. My parents are the hardest working people I have ever known. They were disciplined and had to organize their time in order to efficiently grind and support their family. They did this for several years and never complained. I learned the importance of discipline from them.

Coming from Haiti with a handful of kids to the richest country in the world must have been mind-blowing for my mom and dad. I was born in the U.S. shortly after they had moved here, so I never saw the poverty of the island nation that my older siblings experienced and that my parents came from. Once they had arrived, they could only get low-paying jobs because of their limited English and inexperience, but they made sure that the money that they made lasted as long as it could. My parent's commitment was always to take care of their kids. We were their priority. That meant providing food, shelter, clothing and education for all of us, which was no small undertaking. Achieving that goal drove them to emigrate to the U.S. to give their children a better life than the one that they had in Haiti.

Were my parents disciplined? Did they set goals and grind in order to achieve them? Did they live their truth? Were failures and difficulties feedback for them instead of obstacles that stopped them dead in their tracks? The answer is yes to all of the above. My parents achieved huge goals without even going to college and getting a degree. They took care of their children and brought them to a place where opportunities were available. They learned from their failures and continued to work toward their goals, which they ultimately achieved. They had the discipline to focus all of their power and energy on moving to America and providing their children with the opportunity to live better lives.

My parents, as I mentioned earlier, made sure that their kids didn't struggle and miss opportunities like they did. When I was in the fifth grade, my class was planning to go to Washington, DC, on a field trip. It would cost $200 and I knew there was no way my parents could pay that tab. Please keep in mind that $200 in 1997 was a lot of money, especially for a large family like mine. But somehow my mother and father, who earned very little income, managed to discipline themselves to save enough for their youngest son to take that trip with his classmates. They worked extra hours, planned meticulously, and pinched pennies so that I could have a wonderful educational experience. That trip changed my life. I saw a world outside of Connecticut. They set the example for what truly good parenting should be, and I will never forget their love and sacrifice.

What is your goal? To lose weight and work out more? To graduate from college? To become the president of the United States? A singer, a writer, an entrepreneur? All of these things are possible with discipline. The individuals who run for a political office position are incredible examples of self-discipline. They know what they want and are willing to work through the day doing everything that is necessary to get people's support for their campaign. Their discipline and habits allow them to travel thousands of miles and give speech after speech to people across the nation every day.

Have you ever heard someone tell you that they had to walk four or five miles to and from school or work every day? We have all probably heard some sort of story about a person's perseverance through their crazy trek to and from a location. But have you ever known anyone who has actually had to make a trek like that? My dad was one of those individuals. He walked an hour to school every day when he was growing up in Haiti. Most days he made this walk without a proper meal, good night's rest or supportive walking shoes, but he disciplined himself to do it because he was determined to learn. He didn't let hunger or exhaustion get in the way of gaining all of the knowledge that school could offer.

The best salesperson, the best student, the best school administrator, the best politician all have discipline in common. Without it, your goals will be almost impossible to secure and your grind will be directionless. Tomorrow morning, when you are brushing your teeth, think of it as one of the first disciplined activities that you execute regularly. You will begin to notice more and more as the day goes on that you actually are no stranger to discipline. Once you understand this about yourself, you will be able to become even more disciplined and those goals that you once thought were so distant and unattainable will be within your grasp. If you can brush your teeth daily, you too can live a disciplined life.

Discipline is the bridge between setting goals and actually accomplishing them. If you analyze the journey of those who are successful, you will see that they are repeating the steps of hundreds of people who came before them in order to achieve their goals.

Anything is possible if you brush your teeth every morning. Just kidding, sort of. Happiness, success, prosperity, joy and anything else you can imagine are all possible for anyone. Set a goal, visualize the results, surround yourself with good people, know your worth, live your truth and be disciplined and you can have whatever you dream of. It's not rocket science, but it is a scientific method of achieving goals.

# Absolutely, Positively!

*Someone else's opinion of you does not have to become your reality.*

*-Les Brown*

My father always told me that I was the most powerful person on the planet. He also told me that life is full of choices and that I could be anything that I chose to be. Great words from a great man. Obviously, I am not the most powerful person on the planet and we both knew that when he said it. He didn't mean it literally; he meant that I had the potential to achieve anything that I set my mind to regardless of any obstacles that come my way. Hearing this repeatedly throughout my childhood gave me a lot of confidence and motivation to achieve great things.

Who, then, is the most powerful person on the planet? Is it you? Yes! We are all as powerful as we set our minds to be. We all need to know this truth. Each one of us has the power and the strength of mind to achieve any goal and overcome any obstacle. We simply don't recognize our real value. Most of us don't know the power that lies dormant inside of us. Most of us haven't reached our full potential or tapped into our immense strengths and capabilities. Unfortunately, most of us never will because we haven't developed true self-confidence.

We have grown up thinking that we will reach an average level of success, or just never amount to much because we are not worthy. People from one generation to another, caught up in the continuum of self-depravation, never evolve as they could because they are too busy living the existence to which they felt they were predestined. Nothing is predestined except for death and taxes. Once you know your worth and proceed in the direction you choose, nothing can stop you. Nothing!

People who think they have no value are in a very tough position. If you feel worthless, then you probably believe other people see you that way as well. That is not a very healthy mindset to have. The difficult part is convincing yourself that you are, in fact, valuable. This can be a steep hill to climb on your own, but it can be made easier if you have someone in your circle of friends who can push you to become a better person. Just as my friend Zena saw something valuable in me and pushed me toward an opportunity to better myself. There is something in each and every individual and that is value. That value looks different in each person.

When the CEO fired me for asking for financial help to go back to school, I didn't get mad. I was a little surprised and disappointed, but I wasn't angry with him. I didn't feel sorry for myself either, even though I was out of a job. I understood my worth and I wouldn't let the CEO or anyone else take that away from me. I had value and I knew that I was destined for something greater. I would only go forward and upward from there. When you know your worth, you won't settle for anything less. You will never allow people to take advantage of you. You won't remain stagnant in meaningless jobs or apart of relationships that aren't helping you to become a better person. Knowing your worth gives you the confidence to do what you want and to achieve the goals you set. It gives you the strength to push forward when times are hard.

How does one measure one's worth? Where do you see yourself five or ten years from now? Who are you? These are questions that people have been asking themselves for thousands of years. You don't have to share the answers to any of these questions with others. It is a simple way to promote self-reflection and it is important to know yourself in order to begin to understand your true worth. One way to build your self-worth is by not comparing yourself to other people.

Measuring your accomplishments against those of others is the quickest way to failure and it will just create resentment. You are exactly where you are supposed to be. Live your truth. Focus all of your energy on yourself so that you can reach your goals. Don't believe the hype on social media either. Many online personalities promote a certain lifestyle, but if you are too busy watching them, how does that help you? It just becomes a distraction that will slow your progression down. Another way to build your self-worth is to speak up for yourself. Don't let people belittle you with their words.

Your opinion of yourself is the only thing that truly matters. Get a good understanding of your self-worth so that you can discipline yourself to achieve your goals. Money cannot buy you self-esteem, as this quality comes from within. Humans often think possessions equate to self-worth, but this is absolutely false. Some people are quite happy, even though they have no money because they know their true worth. It is imperative that you understand your value in the world.

What are you worth?

# Live Your Truth

*People love trying to tell you what you need to do for your life and don't even have a plan for theirs. So, if they want to "pop-off", make sure they have a detailed/specific solution. Otherwise, fall back.*

*-President Obama*

Think back to your childhood and all of the times that your parents told you not to do something because the worse imaginable thing might happen. For example, whenever I would cross my eyes my mom would tell me to stop before my eyes got stuck like that forever. Or when my siblings and I would play with sharp objects and my parents would yell, "Stop before you poke your eye out!" But how many of us actually poked our eye out? How many of our eyes actually stayed cross eyed? Not many, I'll bet.

Our parents were being overly protective and we should thank them for not allowing us to take unnecessary risks that could have led to danger when we were younger. But now, we are older, and theoretically, in charge of our own lives and risk taking. That doesn't mean that we all have to be fire eaters, lion trainers or knife throwers at the circus to satisfy our yen for adventure. Those are pretty risky endeavors and the few people who are drawn to those professions are more than enough. There are plenty of risks that we can take while still continuing to move forward toward our goals.

When I decided to go to JCSU in Charlotte, North Carolina, many people tried to talk me out of it. They said that it was too expensive and too far away from home. Some told me that I would never finish school and that I was better off attending a local state college. They figured I could stay at home and save money on rent, and be close to family and friends if I ever needed help. I took this as people basically wanting me to play it safe and I disagreed. I recall visiting a close friend in prison the day before I went away. That friend pretty much didn't support the idea of me leaving Connecticut to go down south for school and was extremely vocal about the mistake that I was about to make. I was so angry, and to be quite frank, fed up with so many individuals not supporting my goal that I walked out of the visiting room. I wanted to live my own truth, and had to realize that not everyone will see your truth for what it is worth.

I moved to North Carolina and enrolled in JCSU, and it was one of the best decisions of my entire life! I would like to say that it was easy, but the opposite was true. Leaving the comfort of my home in Connecticut and saying goodbye to my wonderful parents and siblings was not an easy thing to do. I really missed them. I missed the joking around and the laughter, and I missed being near the people I grew up with and loved so dearly. But in order to achieve my goals, I knew that I needed to leave my comfort zone and expand my horizons.

After the excitement of my first few weeks on campus had died down, the reality of my big move hit me and I realized that things were going to be okay. There were a few challenges here and there, but I got through them as my first year in school progressed. I felt vindicated in my decision to go to a school hundreds of miles away from home, even though my family was worried about my safety and welfare. Every morning, I couldn't wait to get out of bed and go to my classes. On your journey to success, you must follow your heart and do what will make **you** happy, regardless of whether your friends and family approve.

Don't waste time on being upset when you don't receive the support that you desire. Instead, use their doubts as motivation. And when you do accomplish that goal, there is no need to say, "I told you so" or throw anything in anyone's face. Just let your actions speak for themselves. As you go through life, you will begin to notice that the doubts from others will never end as long as your grind continues.

Prior to becoming an Assistant Principal, I worked as a Dean of Students for a prestigious educational organization in the city. Many people told me to play it safe by staying with the organization and wait for a position to open up for me to become an Assistant Principal. They dissuaded me from leaving the school that I had worked at for a few years to start a founding school. People said that it was a bad idea and it was too risky. I didn't listen to them and I'm glad that I didn't.

I left my very comfortable position at a school

that was already established and made what I felt was the best move for my career. Though I was surrounded by doubt when I had hoped to receive encouragement, I chose to live my truth by doing what I thought was right. Many people will tell you what *they think* is best for you. However, you must be able to visualize what the future might hold if you make certain choices and have the willpower to live your truth and make the best decision for you. Not for your friends, not for your parents, but for you!

Living your truth doesn't mean that you have to pretend that you are better than everyone else because you are choosing to limit how their opinions affect you. Living your truth just means listening to your "self" and then doing what you believe is the right thing to do in a humble way. Living your truth can manifest itself in different ways based on the individual. But one thing is for sure, no one else will do what is best for you because no one else cares as much as you do. You have to be the one who decides what your truth is and whether you will live it. Sometimes you may have to take risks to do what is best for you and sometimes those risks will fail. When they do, you have to live with it. Sometimes you might lose friends because you decided to live your truth. So if you think living your truth involves taking a risk, just ask yourself, "Is this worth it" Once you have answered that question, it is time to commit to living your truth.

I have seen many of my peers struggle to live their truth because they fear what people may say. Who cares about the opinions of others? If you are a homosexual, come out and live your truth. If you want to pursue a career in a field that you desire instead of becoming what your parents want you to be, respectfully disagree with them and live your truth. Doing so will bring you happiness and the confidence to pursue your dreams. Once I realized my truth, I created an affirmation that I recite daily. I also have my students say it as a mantra every morning before class. You should do the same. The affirmation I use is:

**I am phenomenal**

**and my life matters.**

**I live my truth,**

**and I am**

**destined for**

**greatness.**

Commit to living your truth!

# Knee-Mail

*Be anxious about nothing, but in everything, by prayer and supplication with thanksgiving, let your requests be made known to God.*

*-Philippians 4:5*

My relationship with God is the reason why I am where I am today. My fraternity brother Durrell once told me, "Obas, if God isn't part of the plan, then it doesn't make sense," and he is absolutely right. I believe in God and I pray, and as far back as I can remember, I have always prayed. I am not here to convince you to start praying. I am simply sharing my life experiences in hopes to inspire you.

On the journey to success, it is inevitable that obstacles and adversity will come your way. And when stumbling blocks appear in front of you, I believe that the only way to overcome them is through your faith in God and communicating with Him. Modern technology gives you plenty of easy ways to speak with your friends and family. You can text, e-mail, Skype, FaceTime or even call them. But your friends and family don't always have the answer, and at times, aren't available. When adversity threatens your success and you don't have a ready solution, you have to communicate with God through knee-mail—that is, get down on your knees and pray to the Lord to see you through. I guarantee that unlike family and friends, He will always be available.

I think back on my time in college. I had the support of my friends and family, but ultimately, it was prayer that allowed me to make it through my trials and tribulations. It was old-fashioned knee-mail that saw me through. It was God who held my hand and guided me through those obstacles that were once in between me and the dais to receive my diploma. I have been using knee-mail my entire life. I think back to my childhood. I remember when I was twelve years old and one of my brothers got shot in his leg. I vividly recall hearing the gunshots being fired outside of my window.

Fortunately, he survived but it was a very hard time for my family. It was tough for me to focus in school because our entire family was worried about his wellbeing. My parents invited some of our church family over to the house to pray with us. I prayed for guidance and clarity because I couldn't fathom why someone was trying to kill my brother. Communicating with the Lord was the only way that I was able to get through this difficult time.

Recently, one of my good friends from college passed away. When my fraternity brother Rob called me and told me the news, I was in utter disbelief and confusion. Why? How? I immediately dropped down to my knees and started speaking with the Lord. The only entity that would be able to answer my questions. So many people were affected by this tragic event, but the common denominator was that everyone remained in prayer.

During my freshman year in high school, times got really hard and my family was evicted from our apartment. We stayed with a family friend for about a month until my parents were able to secure another place for us to live. I recall this part of my life vividly. My spirit was not broken, nor was I defeated, because I prayed alongside my family. I was in constant communication with God and because of this, I was able to focus in school and not resort to making excuses or poor choices. I survived the hard times through prayer and never lost my faith. It's tough to stay strong when life is giving you bumps and blows— when you lose your job, or your parents are in the process of getting a divorce, or you can't find employment, or you can't pay your rent for the month. This is when you need to use knee-mail and say to yourself, "**It is possible; I can make it. I'm going to get through this. I won't allow this to get the best of me**."

The good thing about knee-mail is that it also works when you are in pursuit of greatness, not only when you are in your dark hour. I don't pray to God to give me a brand-new Mercedes or handmade Italian shoes, although those things are very nice and I appreciate the craftsmanship. Instead, I pray for guidance, vision to see things that I normally wouldn't, articulacy, knowledge, forgiveness, direction, patience and understanding. Through these qualities, I will be able to gain wisdom, which will allow me to be successful and make better life decisions.

Have you ever checked the durability of a bench in a park before sitting down on it? Probably not. You don't even think twice about it, as you have faith that the bench will hold you up and you won't fall down. You have faith in the structural integrity of that bench. Over the years, your faith has developed into a conviction; a knowing, so to speak, that the bench will always be there to hold you up, no matter what.

The bench sitters know that they will never fall to the ground. Of course, having the bench collapse under them never occurs to them. It's interesting how people can have that kind of unshakable faith in an inanimate object but not in God. Just like that bench, when I communicate with God through knee-mail, I have faith that he will see me through every trial, guide me through every decision I make, and order my steps to success. I have faith that I will not fall and that God will hold and protect me.

Without God in my life, I would be like a ship blown off course with a broken rudder. I want to feel that I am walking in God's light and love every minute of every day. Using knee-mail allows me to be happier, less stressed and more fulfilled. I have strong faith and when it comes down to it, I thoroughly and unapologetically believe in myself because I believe in

God. As the book of Philippians 4:3 says, "I can do all things through Christ, who strengthens me." #Kneemail

# Give Thanks

*In everything give thanks; for this is God's will for you in Jesus Christ.*

*-I Thessalonians 5:18*

My life's motto is to Give Thanks. I am grateful for all of my life experiences that have made me who I am today. This frame of mind was confirmed one chilly afternoon while I was returning home from work. As I was walking on Broadway in Harlem, a homeless man asked for a dollar to buy something to eat. I brushed passed and ignored him. Immediately afterwards, I tripped on my own feet and almost fell.

In the motion of saving myself from falling, I just so happened to stare at my shoes. The shoes that I was wearing cost $235. I once wore Payless shoes that cost $9.99. I realized that my shoes cost more than 200 times what that poor man was asking from me. *God has an amazing way of getting your attention.* I turned around and walked back to the man. I bought him groceries and a metro card. Once we left C-Town, he said, "Thank you." I said, "No, thank you!"

Simply put, I give thanks because I don't forget where I have come from. There was a time that I was thirsty and someone gave me a cup of water to drink. There was a time that I had fallen and someone lifted me up. There were countless times that I needed a helping hand and there was someone who came during my time of need. Many individuals have contributed to my development and helped me to be the successful man that I am today. As you climb the mountain to success, you must always remain humble and remember your origins. So when I say give thanks, I'm simply saying that I remember where I come from and I am grateful for the experiences life has brought me.

My interaction with this homeless man, or the *angel* that God sent down to Earth to help humble me, changed my life. I realized that no matter how difficult things may seem, there is always someone out there who is struggling just a little bit more than me. Someone might not have water to drink or to shower with. Someone might not have a warm meal to eat or clean clothes to put on their back. Your job is to pay it forward in whatever way you can. This is why I give thanks every day of my life and as I continue to pursue my dreams and goals, I remember this to keep me grounded. I also give thanks for the obstacles that I encounter, for it is through these challenges that I grow as an individual. Giving thanks is a lifestyle; it should be second nature. It is important not only for the balance of things, but for your success and prosperity as well.

When is the last time you gave thanks?

# Success Is Yours

*Keep working hard and you can get anything that you want. If God gave you the talent, you should go for it. But don't think it's going to be easy. It's hard!*

-AALIYAH

And this is the final chapter where I will make sure everything that has been laid out sticks not only in your mind but in the deepest core of your soul. If you have read up to this point in the book, it means that you are committed to making a change. Change is difficult and not everyone can say that they are open to the thought of change... yet you can. I respect you for that! But it's time to make this transitory reading experience a life changing event.

I want to reinforce that you *already* have everything that you need. And by 'already' I'm talking about the intangible qualities that may be dormant inside of you at the moment. These qualities should, must, and will be awakened... by you.

I have shared with you some of my life experiences and the process that I have used towards achieving my goals. If you feel compelled, use these pages as pieces of advice for your journey. You can do it. If I can do it, so can you! You can start achieving goals at any point in your life, whether you are young, middle aged or in your retirement years. Age ain't nothing but a number! It doesn't matter your gender, how much money you make or how many skills you have under your belt; you can achieve your dreams if you have the willpower and discipline to pursue them.

Just always remember trial and error is the mother of its discovery. The most successful people on earth went through a similar process. **Focus on the best actions you can do today**. 'Live in day-tight compartments' as good ol' Dale Carnegie said. Go to bed with a deep inner feeling that you have done *everything* that was in your power to get closer to your goal that day.

Sometimes you will fail and some days you won't be able to go to bed with that feeling of accomplishment. Use your not-so-good days as a learning experience that will give you incredible knowledge about yourself, your emotions, and your thought process. Many of us tend to be discouraged when spectacular results are not attained within a short period of time. We live in a microwave society where we want everything now. But we lack the understanding that success is a process and accomplishing your goals will take time.

Repeated actions over an extended period of time are the solid foundation where remarkable feats are accomplished. If you want to become great at a particular skill or profession, five to twelve hours of committed daily practice done over a period of 10 years is sure to help you achieve that goal. You will notice that, eventually, there is no need to convince yourself that you will be successful because your killer daily practice and commitment will naturally give you this deep rooted belief.

As it has happened to the vast majority of us,

self-doubt will sometimes be your journey companion in the beginning stages. Despair not. Be relentless with your self-talk. Gain as much awareness as you can in regards to the positive thoughts that go through your mind. Intentionally repeat thoughts that are confidence builders. Insist on this as long as it is necessary. Another killer way to ensure self-doubt is eventually erased from your mind is to **only put your focus on people who succeed**.

Listen to their interviews, watch their speeches, read books written by them, learn all of the steps that they took to get where they are. By focusing only on successful people you will begin to link similar traits and thought patterns that they have. Whatever we read or watch is repeated several times in our mind throughout the day.

You will begin to notice that maybe you watched some video or read a post in the morning and you find yourself thinking about it later on in the day. Our mind is an echoing machine and everything that comes in through our eyes and ears will certainly affect our actions. Be cognizant of the messages that you are consciously feeding your brain and ensure that the positive outweighs the negative.

Friend, this is the time where you succeed. I have laid out some steps and I know that you certainly have everything that it takes to turn them into a lifestyle. My best advice to you is to understand that everything of worth in life is not easy to achieve. Nature is wise and has created worthy things as not easily achievable, because **difficulty brings out the necessary #character to achieve them.** Character, ultimately, is what will guide you while you are on **The Grind!**

#ThePowerOfBelief

#SetGoals

#ItsTime

#Visualize

#FailureisFeedback

#SurroundYourselfwithGoodPeople

#ThePowerofSelfDiscipline

#AbsolutelyPositively

#LiveYourTruth

#KneeMail

#GiveThanks

#SuccessisYours

**#TheGrind**

Sincerely,

Mr. Obas

# THE GRIND

# Meet the Author

Simon Obas is a young professional who has embarked on an amazing journey. Born in the United States, he is one of ten children of hard-working immigrant parents. He is a Johnson C. Smith University graduate, a Fordham University graduate with a Masters in Social Work, and is currently pursuing a doctoral degree from Fordham University in Educational Leadership, and is the founding Assistant Principal of a NYC high school. Simon has beaten the odds and has accomplished many challenging goals, while still under the age of 30. He hopes that his life-long journey will inspire others to move forward and achieve their goals, whatever they may be.

# THE GRIND

# The Grind

*Lessons from the Past, Wisdom for the Present*

@obas9
TheGrind1906@gmail.com
#TheGrind

51743469R00059

Made in the USA
Charleston, SC
01 February 2016